It's Not Fair

Written by Brian Moses
Illustrated by Mike Gordon

sundance

Kid-to-Kid Books

Red Set	Green Set	Blue Set	Yellow Set
I Feel Angry	I Feel Bored	I Feel Bullied	Excuse Me!
I Feel Happy	I Feel Jealous	I Feel Frightened	I Don't Care!
I Feel Lonely	I Feel Shy	I Feel Sad	I'll Do It!
It's Not Fair	I Feel Worried	Why Wash?	It Wasn't Me!

This edition published
in North America by
Sundance Publishing
P.O. Box 1326
234 Taylor Street
Littleton, MA 01460

First published in 1997 by
Wayland Publishers Limited

Copyright © 1997 Wayland Publishers Limited

ISBN 0-7608-3918-2

Printed in Canada

In the corner today,
we're talking about

things that aren't fair.

This way to Kids Corner

3

When something isn't fair,

I feel like a bee that can't find a flower.

I feel like a big cat trapped in a small cage.

4

I feel like yelling at someone.

When something isn't fair,

I march out
of the room.

SQUEAK!

I slam the door.

I stomp up the stairs.

7

When my big sister gets new sneakers
and I don't,

it's not fair.

When my friend gets to go
to the movies to see cartoons,
but I can't go,

it's not fair.

When everyone else is picked
to play soccer,
and I'm not,

it's not fair.

I even scored a goal
in the last game.

That makes it
<u>really</u> not fair!

When everyone else can go on the big slide at the fair, and I can't,

it's not fair.

"You can go on the slide when you're older." That's what my parents say.

When my brother won't let me
use the computer,
even when it's my turn,

it's not fair.

"Let me have a turn
or I'll SCREAM!"

Even grown-ups sometimes think life isn't fair.

Why don't I ever win the lottery? It just isn't fair.

When I say, "It's not fair,"
Dad says, "You should be
thankful for what you have."

"When I was a boy . . . " he starts off.
Then he tells me just how little he had!

Sometimes I see
that I'm better off
than some other people.

My big sister thinks it isn't fair
when she has to do homework
and I don't.

24

My friends all say I'm lucky
when I get to go
on a fun vacation.

It's **<u>not</u>** fair!

My dog thinks it isn't fair
when we all go out
and leave him alone in the house.

I can tell
by the sad look
on his face.

When was the last time
you heard someone say,
"It's not fair!"?

Maybe that someone was you.

Set a timer for one minute. Say as many words as you can that rhyme with *fair*. Have a friend write down the words as you say them. Use the words to write a poem about being fair.

The poor dog on page 27 has been left home by his family, and *it's not fair!* Help him tell how he feels. Write a letter from the dog to his family.

Look at the "sound" words on pages 6, 7, and 17. These words stand for noises. Can you think of other sound words? Create a collage using only sound words. Look in other books for ideas.

30

Solve these riddles:
1. I'm a compound word on page 23. What word am I? **2.** I rhyme with hour. I'm on page 4. What word am I? Make up riddles for other words in the book. Ask a friend to solve your riddles.

Fred and Flo are heroes with almost-super powers. They turn *Not Fair* into *Fair*. Make a comic strip about Fred or Flo. Have your hero use his or her powers to make things fair.

my dog

Spot

my house

Other Books to Read

Peter's Chair, by Ezra Jack Keats (HarperCollins, 1967). Peter is not happy with his new baby sister's arrival, especially when his own things are being repainted for her. *30 pages*

The Riddle Streak, by Susan B. Pfeffer (Henry Holt, 1995). Third-grader Amy's older brother always wins—at Ping-Pong, checkers, everything! It's not fair! But then Amy gets an idea. Can she beat him at riddles? *57 pages*

You'll Soon Grow into Them, Titch, by Pat Hutchins (Morrow, 1983). Titch always has to wear hand-me-downs, and it isn't fair. Finally, Titch gets new clothes of his own. *30 pages*

Titch, by Pat Hutchins (Simon and Schuster, 1993). It's not fair that Titch is little and has little things, while everyone else is big. But then Titch gets a little seed that grows and grows and grows! *30 pages*

My Weird Mother, by Wendy Graham (Sundance, 1999). Life can be quite embarrassing with a mother who pushes a dog in a baby carriage and goes everywhere with her pet parrot Presto. It isn't fair that William's mother is so weird. Why can't he have a normal mother like all the other kids? *56 pages*

Looking for Dad, by Ellen Frances (Sundance, 1999). It's just not fair! Why didn't John's mother ask John how he feels about her getting married? John is upset when his mom plans to marry Steve. *64 pages*